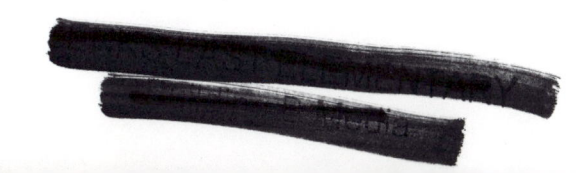

Christmas

I've got a fun activity for you on page 22!

M. C. Hall

Little World Holidays and Celebrations

ROURKE PUBLISHING
www.rourkepublishing.com

© 2011 Rourke Publishing LLC

All rights reserved. No part of this book may be reproduced or utilized in any form or by any means, electronic or mechanical including photocopying, recording, or by any information storage and retrieval system without permission in writing from the publisher.

www.rourkepublishing.com

Photo credits: Rohit Seth/iStockphoto, cover; iStockphoto, 1, 21; Sean Prior/Shutterstock Images, 3, 4; Sean Locke/iStockphoto, 5; AP Images, 6; Mary Terriberry/Shutterstock Images, 7; North Wind Picture Archives/Photolibrary, 8; Christopher Futcher/iStockphoto, 9; Shutterstock Images, 10, 12; Morgan Lane Photography/Shutterstock Images, 11; Martine Oger/Shutterstock Images, 13; Shenjun Zhang/Shutterstock Images, 14; Amy Collins/AP Images, 15; Brian McEntire/iStockphoto, 16; Gene Chutka/iStockphoto, 17; Monkey Business Images/Shutterstock Images, 18; Jason Stitt/Shutterstock Images, 19; Jeffrey Smith/iStockphoto, 20

Editor: Holly Saari

Cover and page design: Kazuko Collins

Content Consultant: Ted Pulcini, PhD, Associate Professor of Religion, Dickinson College, Carlisle, Pennsylvania

Library of Congress Cataloging-in-Publication Data

Hall, Margaret, 1947-
 Christmas / M.C. Hall.
     p. cm. -- (Little world holidays and celebrations)
 Includes bibliographical references and index.
 ISBN 978-1-61590-240-8 (hard cover) (alk. paper)
 ISBN 978-1-61590-480-8 (soft cover)
 1. Christmas--Juvenile literature. I. Title.
 GT4985.5.H35 2011
 394.2663--dc22
                                             2010009912

Rourke Publishing
Printed in the United States of America, North Mankato, Minnesota
033010
033010LP

www.rourkepublishing.com - rourke@rourkepublishing.com
Post Office Box 643328 Vero Beach, Florida 32964

What are these people doing?

They are celebrating Christmas! Each year many people celebrate this holiday on December 25.

Christmas is an important holiday for Christians. Christians are people who practice the **religion** of Christianity.

For Christians, Christmas celebrates the day Jesus was born.

Jesus is an important person to Christians. They believe he is the Son of God and that he came to Earth to save humankind.

Christians have celebrated this holiday for hundreds of years.

Many people celebrate Christmas by going to church. They read the **Bible**, pray, and sing songs.

9

At some churches, people put on plays about the birth of Jesus. The plays help people remember why they celebrate Christmas.

People enjoy other Christmas **traditions** too. Many people decorate Christmas trees with lights and **ornaments**.

Some towns and cities put up huge Christmas trees. Visitors come from far away to see them.

Many families decorate their homes. They hang lights and wreaths on their houses.

Many people send Christmas cards to friends and family. The cards are one way to say Merry Christmas!

People sing special songs, called Christmas **carols**. Some people visit friends and neighbors to sing carols for them.

Before Christmas, some children write letters to Santa Claus. They tell him what gifts they would like for Christmas and whether they have been good that year.

Some families hang stockings on Christmas Eve. Then while everyone is sleeping, Santa Claus visits children's homes to fill the stockings and place gifts under the tree.

During Christmas family and friends spend time with one another. They give gifts and eat a meal together.

Christmas is a time for special treats. During this holiday, there are lots of fun-shaped cookies and candy canes to eat.

People ring bells on corners and in front of stores. They ask people to give money to help those in need.

Christmas is a special holiday for many people around the world.

Craft: Christmas Card

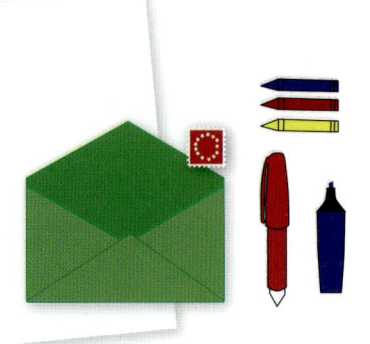

What you need:
- One sheet of construction paper
- Crayons or markers
- Pen
- Envelope
- Stamp

1. Fold one sheet of construction paper in half.

2. On the front write "Merry Christmas." Draw a holiday picture too, such as Santa Claus or a Christmas tree.

3. On the inside of the card, write a message. You can decorate more on the inside too!

4. Put the card in an envelope and send it to someone who celebrates Christmas.

Glossary

Bible (BYE-bul): the holy book of Christianity

carols (KAR-ruhls): joyful songs that are sung at Christmastime

ornaments (OR-nuh-muhnts): small objects hung as decorations

religion (ri-LIJ-uhn): a system of belief, faith, and worship of God or gods

traditions (truh-DISH-uhns): things that are done in the same way every year

Websites to Visit

www.christmas-songs.org/

www.christmastree.org/kids.cfm

www.history.com/topics/christmas/page3

About the Author

M. C. Hall is a former elementary school teacher and an education consultant. As a freelance writer, she has authored teacher materials and more than 100 books for young readers. Hall lives and works in southeastern Massachusetts.